10 Proven Strategies to Grow Your Small Restaurant Business

A Simple Guide to More Customers, More Profit, and a Stronger Restaurant

La Juana Whitmore Consulting

La Juana Whitmore Consulting

Contents

Introduction

Imagine a restaurant that not only draws in new customers but keeps them coming back. A restaurant where pricing, marketing, and customer engagement work in harmony to drive profitability. A restaurant that doesn't just survive industry changes but leverages them to become a neighborhood staple and a growing force in the market. That vision is within reach with the right strategies.

The restaurant industry is at a turning point. Consumer behaviors are shifting faster than ever, technology is redefining the dining experience, and competition is more intense than at any time in history. Small restaurants face an uphill battle. How do you stand out in an era where fast-casual giants and tech-driven delivery services dominate the market?

For independent restaurateurs, success hinges on more than just great food. The landscape demands innovative strategies that capture attention, optimize operations, and create memorable experiences for customers. Those who fail to adapt risk falling behind, but those who embrace change have the opportunity to thrive.

This guide will walk you through the proven methods that small restaurants are using to grow today. From mastering digital marketing to refining customer experiences and optimizing operations, these strategies will equip you with the tools needed to stay ahead of the competition. **It's time to take your restaurant to the next level!**

1. Understanding Your Market: Know Your Customers, Own Your Niche

1. Strategy One

Understanding Your Market: Know Your Customers, Own Your Niche

In an increasingly competitive restaurant landscape, understanding your customers is the foundation for long-term success. The restaurants that thrive are the ones that anticipate customer preferences, leverage data-driven insights, and create a brand identity that stands out in a crowded market. Simply serving great food isn't enough, you need to position your restaurant strategically to attract the right customers and keep them coming back.

Analyzing Local Dining Trends and Customer Preferences

Your restaurant doesn't exist in a vacuum, it's part of a dynamic, ever-changing local dining scene. To build a sustainable business, you need to **stay ahead of shifting customer preferences and food trends** [1] [2] [3].

Monitor Emerging Food Trends in Your Area

- Are diners in your city gravitating toward plant-based options, fusion cuisine, or sustainable eating?

- Is your neighborhood experiencing a rise in fast-casual

dining, delivery-heavy restaurants, or premium fine dining?

- Are customers looking for low-carb, high-protein, or globally inspired flavors?

> **Use Google Trends, social media analytics, and local restaurant reports to track what's gaining popularity. Observing what's working for competitors, and what isn't, can help you position your menu offerings to fill market gaps.**

Listen to What Customers Are Saying

Real-time feedback is gold for understanding diner preferences. Stay engaged by:

- Reading and responding to Yelp, Google, and OpenTable reviews to identify what customers love, and what they don't.

- Running quick social media polls (e.g., "What new dish would you love to see on our menu?").

- Encouraging servers to ask informal questions during table service (e.g., "What's your favorite dish here?" or "What would you love to see more of?").

Keep an Eye on Competitors

- Visit popular local restaurants and analyze what makes them successful.

- Follow their social media and pay attention to customer

engagement.

- Note pricing strategies, menu innovations, and promotional tactics.

> **Being aware of what's happening around you allows you to differentiate your restaurant rather than imitate others.**

Leveraging Data to Identify Your Most Profitable Customers

Knowing your best customers, not just your general audience, allows you to make smarter marketing and menu decisions. Instead of chasing broad demographics, focus on who drives the most revenue for your restaurant [4] [5] [6].

Use Customer Relationship Management (CRM) Tools

Technology makes it easier than ever to analyze customer behaviors. Platforms like Toast, Square, and OpenTable track:

- Frequency of visits (Who are your repeat customers?)

- Average spend per visit (Which guests order premium items?)

- Menu favorites (What dishes keep bringing them back?)

With this data, you can personalize marketing campaigns, offering exclusive promotions or loyalty rewards to your highest-value customers.

Implement a Loyalty Program

Loyalty programs not only boost repeat business but also provide valuable customer insights.

- Offer points-based rewards (e.g., "BOGO: Earn 1 point per $1 spent—get $10 off after 100 points!").

- Provide VIP experiences (e.g., "Exclusive access to new menu tastings for loyalty members").

- Send personalized offers based on past purchases (e.g., "We noticed you love our steak frites—enjoy a free appetizer with your next order!").

Identify High-Value Customers and Cater to Them

Not all customers contribute equally to your bottom line. Find out:

- Who orders high-margin items (specialty cocktails, premium entrees)?

- Who dines frequently and brings friends/family?

- Who leaves positive reviews and engages on social media?

Once you identify your best customers, reward them and build stronger relationships to encourage even more visits.

Crafting a Unique Brand Identity That Stands Out

Today, restaurants that succeed don't just serve food, they tell a story and create an experience. Your brand identity is the emotional connection customers have with your restaurant [7] [8] [9].

Define Your Core Message

- What's your restaurant's story?

- What makes your dining experience different from competitors?

- What emotions should customers associate with your brand? (e.g., cozy and nostalgic, energetic and trendy, upscale and refined)

> **Your mission statement and brand voice should be consistent across your menu, social media, website, and in-person experience.**

Design a Distinct Visual Identity

A cohesive visual brand makes your restaurant instantly recognizable. Invest in:

- A professional logo that reflects your concept.

- A consistent color palette used in your website, menus, and decor.

- A stylized plating and presentation style that stands out

on social media.

Infuse Your Personality Into Your Marketing

People don't connect with businesses, they connect with stories, emotions, and people. Your brand should have a personality that resonates with your audience.

- Are you playful and fun? Use a witty and engaging tone.

- Are you elegant and high-end? Use polished language and refined imagery.

- Are you community-focused? Share stories about your local partnerships and behind-the-scenes moments.

Stay Consistent Across All Touchpoints

Your brand identity should be reflected in *everything*, from your interior design and staff uniforms to your social media tone and menu descriptions.

- If you run a farm-to-table concept, your Instagram feed should showcase fresh ingredients and local farm visits.

- If you're a trendy cocktail bar, your website should have a sleek, modern aesthetic with vibrant photography.

- If you market as a family-friendly pizzeria, your social media should highlight family dining moments and kids' meal deals.

Final Thoughts

Understanding your market is the foundation for every successful restaurant strategy. The most successful restaurants will be those that stay ahead of shifting food trends, leverage customer data for smarter marketing, and build an authentic, recognizable brand identity. By keeping a close eye on local dining preferences, analyzing customer behaviors, and crafting a unique experience that resonates with your audience, you create a restaurant that not only attracts customers but keeps them coming back. A strong market strategy isn't just about following trends, it's about positioning your restaurant as the go-to dining destination in your community. When you truly know your audience and own your niche, your restaurant becomes more than just a place to eat; it becomes a brand that diners connect with and remember.

1. Roy, D., & Spiliotopoulou, E. (2022). Restaurant analytics: Emerging practice and research opportunities.

2. Espinoza Mercado, O. A. (2022). Innovation and Customer-Centric Analysis: Restaurant industry.

3. Tsubiks, O., & Kešelj, V. (2018). A Market Analytics Approach to Restaurant Review Data.

4. Swink, M., Hu, K., & Zhao, X. (2022). Analytics applications, limitations, and opportunities in restaurant supply chains.

5. Bilgihan, A., Seo, S., & Choi, J. (2018). Identifying restaurant satisfiers and dissatisfiers: Suggestions from online reviews.

6. Jenkins, W. Y. (2015). Marketing strategies for profitability in small independent restaurants.

7. Sharma, B., Arora, R., & Kharub, M. (2021). Critical success factors affecting the restaurant industry: Insights from restaurant managers.

8. Bowden, J. (2009). Customer engagement: A framework for assessing customer-brand relationships: The case of the restaurant industry.

9. Elkhwesky, Z., & Castañeda-García, J. A. (2023). A systematic and critical review of restaurants' business performance: Future directions for theory and practice.

Oysters, champagne mignonette
Gougeres topped with light cheese cream

Kangaroo saucissons, smoked trout rillette, chicken liver parfait
Baguette, country loaf and caramelized butter
**Domaine Jousset – Exilé Rosé Pet Nat 2016 – Vin de
France**

2. Menu Optimization: More Than Just Great Food

Tarragon
Pierre Cotton – Le Pré 2017 – AOC Beaujel

Mandarin and burnt honey opera
Financier madeleines

2. Strategy Two

Menu Optimization: More Than Just Great Food

Your menu is more than just a list of dishes, it's a powerful marketing tool that can influence customer decisions, maximize profits, and define your restaurant's identity. A well-optimized menu balances customer preferences, profitability, and operational efficiency to create an experience that keeps guests coming back. Today, restaurants must focus on strategic menu design, data-driven pricing, and streamlined offerings to remain competitive.

How to Design a Menu That Boosts Profitability

A well-designed menu doesn't just make food look appealing, it guides customer choices toward high-margin items while ensuring an enjoyable dining experience [1] [2] [3].

Highlight High-Profit Items Strategically

Menu psychology plays a huge role in influencing what customers order and how much they spend. Use design techniques to subtly direct attention to your most profitable dishes:

- Placement Matters: Customers' eyes are naturally drawn to certain areas of the menu. High-margin items should be placed in the top-right corner or boxed for emphasis.

- Descriptive Language Sells: Instead of listing "Grilled Chicken Sandwich," make it "Smoky Mesquite-Grilled Chicken on a Toasted Brioche Bun." Studies show detailed descriptions increase sales by up to 27%.

- Use Visual Cues: Small icons (like a chef's recommendation star or a "customer favorite" badge) draw attention to dishes you want to sell more of.

- Strategic Pricing Anchoring: Placing a high-priced item next to a mid-tier one makes the mid-tier item look like a "good deal," increasing its sales.

Use Seasonal and Local Ingredients

A seasonal menu not only enhances freshness but also helps reduce ingredient costs by taking advantage of locally available produce.

> **Consumers are more conscious of sustainability and quality than ever before.**

- Rotate menu items quarterly to reflect the best seasonal ingredients.

- Highlight local farm partnerships on your menu and social media.

- Offer limited-time dishes to create urgency and encourage repeat visits.

The Psychology Behind Menu Pricing and Layout

The way you structure and price your menu impacts how much customers spend. Restaurants that use menu psychology can increase average ticket sizes without raising costs [4][5][6].

Avoid Currency Signs and Round Pricing

- Studies show that removing the dollar sign ($) makes customers less focused on the price and more focused on the food. Instead of listing $12.99, just write 12.99 for a cleaner, upscale feel.

- Avoid using pricing columns, as they encourage customers to compare prices instead of dishes. Instead, list prices subtly at the end of the description.

Offer Bundled Pricing and Add-Ons

- Bundle complementary items (e.g., a burger, fries, and drink for one price) to increase per-ticket revenue while offering perceived value.

- Encourage add-ons by suggesting premium options (e.g., "Upgrade your fries to truffle parmesan for +$3").

The Power of the Decoy Effect

> **The decoy effect is a pricing strategy that makes one option seem like a "better deal."**

If you sell two portion sizes, add a third, slightly more expensive one that makes the middle option look like the best value. This often nudges customers toward higher-priced items.Example:

- Small Pasta - $12

- **Medium Pasta - $15 (Best Value)**

- Large Pasta - $19

Most diners will choose the medium because it seems like the best deal compared to the high-priced large portion.

Streamlining Your Offerings for Efficiency and Customer Satisfaction

A complicated menu overwhelms customers and slows down kitchen operations. Simplifying your menu enhances efficiency, ensures consistency, and increases profitability [7] [8].

Reduce Menu Size Without Losing Variety

A well-optimized menu focuses on quality over quantity.

> **Too many choices can lead to decision fatigue, making it harder for customers to order and increasing table turn times.**

- Identify underperforming dishes and remove low-margin, low-sales items.

- Keep a balanced variety of customer favorites, signature dishes, and seasonal specials.

- Ensure ingredients can be used across multiple dishes to reduce waste and inventory costs.

Offer Customization Without Overcomplication

Instead of offering dozens of individual items, allow for customizable options that don't disrupt kitchen efficiency.

- Example for a Burger Menu: Offer one base burger with customizable toppings rather than five different burger variations.

- Example for a Salad Menu: Allow customers to choose their protein and dressing rather than listing separate salads with the same base ingredients.

Use Data to Optimize Menu Performance

Your POS (point-of-sale) system is a goldmine of information. Use data to track:

- Which items sell the most and least?

- What are the highest-margin dishes?

- When do customers order certain items the most?

Adjust your menu accordingly to maximize profit without sacrificing customer experience.

Final Thoughts

A well-optimized menu boosts profitability, improves customer experience, and streamlines restaurant operations. By designing a menu that highlights high-margin items, using smart pricing strategies, and simplifying offerings, you ensure that customers enjoy their dining experience while your restaurant maximizes revenue. The best menus are data-driven, visually appealing, and structured to guide customer choices effortlessly. The key is to find the perfect balance between creativity, efficiency, and profitability, because in the restaurant industry, the right menu can make all the difference.

---

1. Webb, T., Ma, J., & Cheng, A. (2023). Variable Pricing in Restaurant Revenue Management: A Priority Mixed Bundle Strategy.

2. Jenkins, W. Y. (2015). Marketing strategies for profitability in small independent restaurants.

3. Lai, H. B. J., & Karim, S. (2023). Do-it-yourself menu management and pricing.

4. Thompson, G. M. (2010). Restaurant Profitability Management: The Evolution of Restaurant Revenue Management.

5. Ozdemir, B., & Caliskan, O. (2014). A Review of Literature on Restaurant Menus: Specifying the Managerial Issues.

6. Phillips, R. L. (2021). Pricing and Revenue Optimization.

7. Raab, C., Mayer, K., & Kim, Y. S. (2009). Price-Sensitivity Measurement: A Tool for Restaurant Menu Pricing.

8. Vives, A., Jacob, M., & Payeras, M. (2018). Revenue Management and Price Optimization Techniques in the Hotel Sector: A Critical Literature Review.

3. Restaurant Marketing That Connects With Your Community

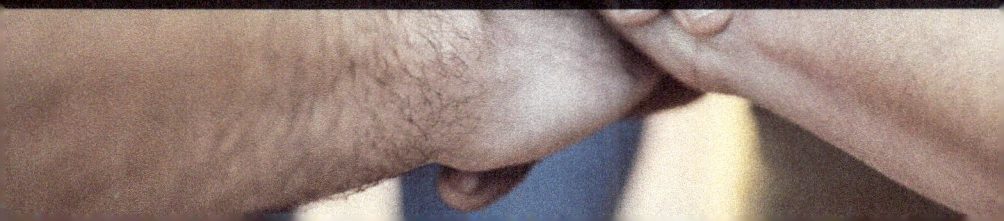

3. Strategy Three

Restaurant Marketing That Connects With Your Community

M arketing your restaurant isn't just about advertising, it's about building relationships. The most successful restaurants are the ones that deeply engage with their local communities, foster brand loyalty, and create experiences that keep customers coming back. Whether through grassroots marketing, hosting community events, or collaborating with local businesses, strong local connections translate into long-term success.

The Power of Grassroots Marketing and Local Partnerships

Grassroots marketing is one of the most cost-effective ways to build a loyal customer base. Instead of relying solely on paid ads, restaurants that embed themselves into their communities can generate consistent foot traffic and turn locals into brand ambassadors [1][2][3][4][5][6].

Partner With Local Organizations and Charities

- Sponsor school fundraisers, youth sports teams, or community events. This builds goodwill and strengthens brand loyalty.

- Collaborate with nonprofits by donating a portion of sales on certain days (e.g., "Dine with us on Tuesdays, and we'll donate 10% to the local food bank").

- Offer a discount for community heroes like teachers, healthcare workers, and first responders to show appreciation while attracting repeat business.

Become a Recognized Local Staple

- Attend local farmers' markets, street fairs, and food festivals to introduce your brand to potential customers.

- Offer exclusive deals for neighborhood residents (e.g., "Show your ID for 15% off every Sunday!").

- Partner with local influencers and food bloggers to organically promote your restaurant to their audiences.

Encourage Word-of-Mouth Marketing

> **People trust recommendations from friends, family, and local community members more than any ad campaign.**

Create opportunities for organic buzz by:

- Launching a referral program (e.g., "Bring a friend and both get a free appetizer!").

- Offering loyalty rewards that encourage frequent visits.

- Incentivizing customers to leave reviews or post about their dining experience on social media.

Hosting Community Events to Boost Visibility

> **Events are a powerful way to attract new customers, increase foot traffic, and create memorable dining experiences.**

By hosting unique, engaging events, you can position your restaurant as a gathering place for the community [7] [8].

Host Special Theme Nights

- Trivia Nights: Partner with a local trivia host and offer themed food specials.

- Live Music or Open Mic Nights: Showcase local musicians and artists while drawing in new crowds.

- Cultural or Seasonal Events: Celebrate local holidays, cuisines, or traditions with special menus and decor.

Offer Interactive Dining Experiences

- Cooking Classes or Chef's Table Events: Let customers get hands-on with the culinary experience, offering a behind-the-scenes look at how their favorite dishes are made.

- Food and Wine Pairing Dinners: Partner with a local vineyard or brewery to create a curated dining experience.

- Tasting Events for New Menu Items: Invite loyal customers to preview and vote on new dishes, making them feel like insiders.

Use Events as a PR and Social Media Opportunity

- Livestream events on Instagram and Facebook to engage customers who couldn't attend in person.

- Post behind-the-scenes content (e.g., "Getting ready for our first-ever chef's table dinner!").

- Send out a press release to local media about upcoming events to attract additional exposure.

Collaborating With Local Businesses for Cross-Promotions

Teaming up with other small businesses in your community can expand your reach, attract new customers, and strengthen your brand.

Cross-promotions allow both businesses to benefit from shared audiences and mutual referrals [9] [10].

Partner With Coffee Shops, Breweries, and Bakeries

- Offer a "Dine & Drink" experience with a local brewery, pairing craft beers with your menu items.

- Work with a local coffee shop or bakery to serve their products at your restaurant in exchange for them promoting your business.

- Collaborate on a seasonal dish or limited-edition menu item (e.g., "Pumpkin spice dessert featuring Bloomington Café espresso").

Create Exclusive Local Business Discounts

- Partner with gyms, yoga studios, or wellness centers to offer discounts (e.g., "Show your gym membership for 10% off healthy menu options").

- Offer local office workers a lunchtime discount to drive weekday traffic.

- Run a "Shop Local" promotion where customers can show a receipt from a partnering business to receive a discount at your restaurant.

Cross-Promote on Social Media

- Feature each other's businesses in Instagram Stories and posts.

- Run a giveaway collaboration (e.g., "Win a dinner for two at La Cocina Bonita plus get a free dessert from Bloomington Bakery!").

- Share customer experiences that showcase both businesses (e.g., "We stopped by Minnie Eatery for dinner after a fun afternoon at Westman Art Gallery!").

Final Thoughts

Marketing that focuses on community engagement, events, and local partnerships helps turn first-time visitors into lifelong customers. Restaurants that actively participate in their neighborhoods, build relationships with other businesses, and create meaningful experiences will stand out. Instead of just promoting your menu, focus on building connections, because when people feel emotionally invested in your restaurant, they're more likely to return, bring friends, and share their experiences. A strong local presence, combined with smart partnerships and unforgettable events, transforms a restaurant into a community staple.

---

1. Toshmirzaev, D., Ahn, Y., & Kiatkawsin, K. (2022). The effect of corporate social responsibility on trustful relationship, supportive communication intention, and brand loyalty of ethnic halal restaurants.

2. Aleksejeva, A. M. (2015). Relationship marketing in customer service–oriented business segment: Development of trust as a marketing tool: Case study of the restaurant.

3. Mattila, A. S. (2001). Emotional bonding and restaurant loyalty.

4. Hubbard, L. J. (2018). Small Business Restaurant Marketing Strategies for Sustainability.

5. Bowden-Everson, J. L. H., & Dagger, T. S. (2013). Engaging customers for loyalty in the restaurant industry: The role of satisfaction, trust, and delight.

6. Chang, K. C. (2013). How reputation creates loyalty in the restaurant sector.

7. McDonnell, J., Beatson, A., & Huang, C. H. (2011). Investigating relationships between relationship quality, customer loyalty and cooperation: An empirical study of convenience stores' franchise chain systems.

8. Cho, M., Bonn, M. A., Han, S. J., & Kang, S. (2018). Partnership strength and diversity with suppliers: Effects upon independent restaurant product innovation and performance.

9. Robinson, C., Abbott, J. A., & Shoemaker, S. (2005). Recreating Cheers: An analysis of relationship marketing as an effective marketing technique for quick-service restaurants.

10. Yoo, M., & Bai, B. (2013). Customer loyalty marketing research: A comparative approach between hospitality and business journals.

4. Social Media and Digital Presence: Making Every Post Count

4. Strategy Four

Social Media and Digital Presence: Making Every Post Count

Today, a strong digital presence isn't optional, it's essential. Restaurants that embrace the latest social media trends, engage with customers through short-form video, and encourage user-generated content will thrive in a highly competitive market. Your restaurant's digital strategy should focus on creating content that is engaging, shareable, and designed for conversions.

The must-have platforms for restaurants

Not all social media platforms are created equal. Restaurants must be strategic about where they invest time and effort. Here's a breakdown of the most critical platforms for growing your restaurant's brand and attracting customers [1] [2].

TikTok: The King of Food Trends

TikTok remains the most influential platform for viral food trends, with millions of users engaging in recipe challenges, food reviews, and behind-the-scenes kitchen clips. Restaurants that leverage TikTok's algorithm can rapidly increase brand awareness by showcasing unique menu items, limited-time specials, or even playful chef challenges.

- Post short, visually appealing "sizzle" videos of signature dishes.

- Use trending audio clips and hashtags (e.g., #FoodTok, #HiddenGems, #ViralEats).

- Engage with influencers and food bloggers to boost visibility.

Instagram: The Visual Showstopper

Instagram continues to be a powerhouse for restaurant marketing, but now, Reels and Stories dominate over static posts. This platform is where restaurants can cultivate a strong brand aesthetic while maintaining high engagement.

- Use Instagram Reels to highlight food prep, plating techniques, and behind-the-scenes moments.

- Post daily Stories with interactive polls (e.g., "Which new dish should we add?").

YouTube Shorts: The Secret Weapon for SEO

While TikTok and Instagram dominate the short-form video world, YouTube Shorts is an underrated yet powerful tool for restaurant marketing. Google prioritizes YouTube content in search results, meaning your Shorts can help you rank higher when potential customers search for restaurants in your area.

- Post 15-60 second videos showcasing signature dishes,

chef tips, or customer testimonials.

- Optimize titles and descriptions with SEO keywords like Best brunch in Bloomington" or "Top pizza spots near me."

- Add playlists featuring categories like "Behind the Scenes" or "How It's Made."

Facebook: Still Relevant for Local Marketing

Facebook may not be as trendy, but local marketing and community engagement are where it excels. Restaurants should leverage Facebook Groups, Events, and targeted ads to stay connected with loyal customers.

- Create Facebook Events for special promotions, new menu launches, and live music nights.

- Post in local foodie groups to attract nearby customers.

- Run geo-targeted ads featuring special offers for users within a specific radius.

Engaging with customers through short-form video content

> **Short-form video remains the #1 most engaging content format, and restaurants that use it effectively will see higher engagement, stronger brand loyalty, and more foot traffic.**

The key is to create snackable, high-energy videos that capture attention within the first three seconds [3][4][5][6].

Behind-the-Scenes Kitchen Content

People love to see what happens behind the counter. Share quick-cut clips of:

- Chefs preparing a signature dish in 30 seconds.

- "Day in the life" videos showcasing restaurant prep and rush hours.

- Unique or secret menu items coming to life.

ASMR and Satisfying Food Videos

ASMR-style videos, where the sizzling of a steak, the crunch of a taco, or the drizzle of syrup is amplified, are incredibly engaging and shareable.

> **Sound and texture play a massive role in food marketing.**

- Use high-quality audio to enhance sensory appeal.

- Film close-up, slow-motion shots of food being prepared or served.

- Create loopable clips that are satisfying to watch (e.g., cheese pulls, sauce drizzles, or cocktails being shaken).

Interactive Content: Polls, Challenges & Giveaways

Interactivity keeps viewers engaged. Restaurants can use video content to invite participation through:

- Food Challenges: "Can you eat this in under 5 minutes? Try it at Bloomington's Best Burgers!"

- Polls & Q&As: "Would you rather try our spicy new wings or our honey-glazed ribs? Comment below!"

- Giveaways: "Tag a foodie friend for a chance to win a free dinner!"

Encouraging user-generated content and online reviews

> **Nothing builds credibility faster than real customers advocating for your brand.**

User-generated content (UGC) is one of the most effective ways to establish trust, improve organic reach, and convert potential diners into paying customers [7] [8] [9].

Incentivize Customers to Post About Your Restaurant

Encourage diners to share their experiences by offering:

- A small discount or free appetizer for tagging your restaurant in their post.

- A weekly "Best Photo" contest, where the best user-submitted photo gets featured on your Instagram and wins a prize.

- A branded hashtag challenge (e.g., #MyBestBiteAtBubbasBurgers) to encourage more participation.

Repost & Highlight Customer Content

Make your customers feel like VIPs by featuring their content on your social media:

- Repost Instagram Stories where customers have tagged your restaurant.

- Add a "Fan Favorites" highlight reel on Instagram showcasing the best UGC.

- Feature positive reviews in short-form videos with overlay text reading: "What people are saying about us!"

Turn Reviews Into Content

Reviews on Google, Yelp, and TripAdvisor don't have to stay on those platforms. Repurpose them into engaging content by:

- Creating text-overlay videos featuring customer testimonials.

- Making side-by-side reaction videos reading great reviews and showing the dish they're talking about.

- Designing "Thank You" posts featuring five-star reviews to show appreciation for your community.

Final Thoughts

Restaurants that master social media and digital engagement will be the ones that thrive. By focusing on the right platforms, short-form video, and user-generated content, your restaurant can stand out, build a loyal customer base, and turn digital interactions into real-world dining experiences.

The key is to be consistent, engaging, and community-driven, because in the restaurant industry, people don't just buy food; they buy experiences.

---

1. Kulkarni, S. (2025). Role of Social Media Marketing in Food Industry.

2. Lin, I. (2022). TikTok marketing for restaurant business.

3. Eng, S. Y. (2023). The impact of short-form video as electronic word-of-mouth on consumer visit intention: a comparison between TikTok and Instagram.

4. Alghizzawi, M., Alzghoul, A., & Alhanatleh, H. (2024). Short video marketing and consumer engagement: Mediation effect of social sharing.

5. Li, H., & Tu, X. (2024). Who generates your video ads? The matching effect of short-form video sources and destination types on visit intention.

6. Apasrawirote, D., & Yawised, K. (2022). Short-form video content (SVC) engagement and marketing capabilities.

7. Khine, W. L. M. (2024). The impact of media richness, celebrity endorsement, and consumers' engagement of TikTok marketing on their intention to visit restaurants in Thailand.

8. Tran, N. (2023). Digital Marketing plan for Restaurant 64.

9. Li, Z., & Zhang, J. (2023). How to improve destination brand identification and loyalty using short-form videos? The role of emotional experience and self-congruity.

5. Leveraging AI and Automation to Streamline Operations

5. Strategy Five

Leveraging AI and Automation to Streamline Operations

A I and automation are no longer optional for restaurants looking to scale efficiently, they're essential tools for improving productivity, reducing operational costs, and optimizing the customer experience. By integrating AI-driven solutions and automated processes, restaurants can reduce labor-intensive tasks, minimize waste, and enhance service speed and accuracy. From reservations to inventory tracking, technology is transforming restaurant operations, making it easier than ever to manage workflows while keeping customers satisfied.

How AI-driven tools can improve efficiency and reduce costs

Artificial intelligence is revolutionizing the restaurant industry by taking over time-consuming manual tasks and allowing staff to focus on customer experience and food quality. AI-driven solutions enhance operational efficiency while cutting unnecessary costs, leading to better margins and smoother daily operations [1] [2] [3] [4].

AI-Powered Scheduling and Labor Optimization

One of the biggest cost drivers in restaurants is labor. AI-powered scheduling tools like 7shifts, OpenSimSim, and Homebase analyze sales trends and customer foot traffic to:

- Predict peak hours and optimize staff scheduling accordingly.

- Minimize overstaffing during slow periods while ensuring full coverage during rush hours.

- Reduce labor costs by tracking employee productivity and adjusting schedules automatically.

> **Example: An AI scheduling tool notices a pattern of high lunch traffic on Thursdays and automatically adds an extra line cook and two servers to the schedule, preventing slow service and customer dissatisfaction.**

AI-Powered Dynamic Pricing

Some restaurants are experimenting with dynamic menu pricing, similar to airlines and hotels. AI-driven tools adjust pricing based on:

- Time of day (e.g., offering discounts during off-peak hours to attract more customers).

- Ingredient availability (e.g., adjusting menu prices when supplier costs increase).

- Customer demand (e.g., raising the price of a best-selling dish to maximize profit).

This ensures that restaurants stay profitable while staying competitive, offering customers the best prices without cutting into margins.

AI for Customer Insights and Personalization

AI-driven customer analytics tools (like Toast, Square, and Lightspeed) help restaurants:

- Analyze customer behavior to determine popular menu items and ordering habits.

- Personalize promotions by suggesting deals based on customer purchase history.

- Improve loyalty programs by tailoring rewards to individual preferences.

> **Example: A returning customer orders a spicy chicken sandwich three times in a month. AI detects the pattern and automatically sends them a push notification offering a discount on their next spicy chicken sandwich, increasing the likelihood of repeat purchases.**

Using automation for reservations, ordering, and customer service

Automation allows restaurants to operate with greater efficiency while enhancing the customer experience. Whether it's taking reservations, handling online orders, or managing guest interactions, automation tools eliminate manual tasks and reduce human error [5][6][7][8].

Automated Reservation Systems for Seamless Booking

Customers expect an easy, instant way to reserve tables. AI-powered reservation platforms like OpenTable, Resy, and EatApp allow diners to:

- Book tables online without calling the restaurant.

- Receive automatic confirmations and reminders, reducing no-shows.

- Join virtual waitlists during peak hours and get notified when a table is ready.

> **Example: A customer searching for "best brunch spots near me" finds your restaurant on Google and instantly books a table via an AI-powered reservation widget, eliminating the need for a phone call.**

AI-Powered Voice Assistants for Ordering

Voice AI assistants like Google Duplex and Amazon Alexa are enabling hands-free ordering by:

- Taking drive-thru and phone orders with AI-powered voice recognition.

- Recommending add-ons to increase average order value.

- Improving accuracy by eliminating misheard or miswritten orders.

> **Example: A customer places a drive-thru order at an AI-powered kiosk, and the system automatically suggests an upsell: "Would you like to add a side of fries for $2 more?", leading to a higher ticket size.**

AI Chatbots for Instant Customer Support

AI chatbots, integrated into websites and social media, reduce wait times and handle customer inquiries automatically. These bots can:

- Answer frequently asked questions about hours, location, and menu items.

- Process online orders via messaging apps like Facebook Messenger and WhatsApp.

- Manage complaints in real-time, directing customers to the right support channel.

> **Example: A customer sends a DM asking, "Do you have gluten-free options?" and your AI chatbot instantly replies with a list of gluten-free dishes and a link to order online.**

Smart inventory management to minimize waste and maximize profits

Food waste is one of the biggest profit killers in the restaurant industry. Smart inventory management tools track stock levels, predict usage patterns, and reduce food waste, helping restaurants save money while improving sustainability [9].

AI-Driven Inventory Forecasting

Traditional inventory tracking is time-consuming and prone to human error. AI-powered systems like BlueCart, MarketMan, and xtraCHEF analyze:

- Real-time ingredient usage to prevent over-ordering.

- Sales trends to predict how much of each ingredient is needed.

- Expiration dates to ensure food is used before it goes to waste.

> **Example: Your AI inventory system notices that avocados are consistently underused and expiring before they're sold. It suggests reducing avocado orders and offering a temporary avocado-based special to use up existing stock before it spoils.**

Automated Supplier Ordering

Instead of manually placing orders, AI-powered inventory systems automatically reorder ingredients when stock runs low, ensuring the kitchen is always prepared. These systems:

- Connect with suppliers to track availability and pricing.

- Prevent shortages of essential ingredients.

- Reduce manual errors in inventory management.

> **Example: Your kitchen runs low on chicken breasts, and the AI system automatically places an order with your supplier, ensuring there's no disruption to menu offerings.**

Reducing Waste Through Smart Portioning

AI-driven portioning tools help kitchens reduce overuse of ingredients by:

- Standardizing portion sizes to maintain consistency.

- Identifying high-waste menu items and adjusting recipes accordingly.

- Tracking which items are frequently left unfinished and suggesting portion adjustments.

> **Example: Your AI analytics show that customers frequently leave half of their pasta dishes uneaten, prompting a menu adjustment to offer a smaller portion option at a lower price, reducing waste and increasing customer satisfaction.**

Final Thoughts

AI and automation are changing the way restaurants operate, making them more efficient, cost-effective, and customer-friendly. By leveraging AI-driven scheduling, automated ordering, and smart inventory management, restaurants can streamline operations and focus on what truly matters: delivering great food and exceptional service. Restaurants that embrace technology-driven efficiency will not only improve their bottom line but also enhance the overall dining experience, ensuring a smarter, smoother, and more profitable future.

---

1. Tuomi, A., & Ascenção, M. P. (2023). Intelligent automation in hospitality: exploring the relative automatability of frontline food service tasks.

2. Seyitoğlu, F., Atsız, O., & Acar, A. (2025). The role of technology in the future of restaurant labor.

3. Kumar, I., Rawat, J., Mohd, N., & Husain, S. (2021). Opportunities of artificial intelligence and machine learning in the food industry.

4. Yang, L., Henthorne, T. L., & George, B. (2020). Artificial intelligence and robotics technology in the hospitality industry: Current applications and future trends.

5. Berezina, K., Ciftci, O., & Cobanoglu, C. (2019). Robots, artificial intelligence, and service automation in restaurants.

6. Blöcher, K., & Alt, R. (2021). AI and robotics in the European restaurant sector: Assessing potentials for process innovation in a high-contact service industry.

7. Maier, T., & Edwards, K. (2020). Service system design and automation in the hospitality sector.

8. Milton, T. (2024). "Artificial Intelligence Transforming Hotel Gastronomy: An In-depth Review of AI-driven Innovations in Menu Design, Food Preparation, and Customer Interaction."

9. Volyanik, G., & Shutka, S. (2024). Current trends of the implementation of intelligent automated technologies in the sphere of restaurant electronic business.

6. Mastering Online Reviews: Turning Feedback Into Growth

6. Strategy Six

Mastering Online Reviews: Turning Feedback Into Growth

O nline reviews can make or break a restaurant. Whether it's Google Reviews, Yelp, TripAdvisor, or Facebook, customer feedback directly influences dining decisions, search engine rankings, and brand reputation. A well-managed review strategy not only boosts credibility but also helps convert potential customers into loyal diners. Restaurants that actively engage with reviews, both positive and negative, gain trust, improve service quality, and use feedback to refine operations.

Encouraging positive reviews and handling negative ones gracefully

Getting more positive reviews requires a proactive approach; happy customers often don't leave feedback unless prompted, while dissatisfied guests are more likely to share their experience. Here's how to amplify positive reviews while mitigating negative ones [1] [2].

Encourage More Positive Reviews

Ask at the Right Moment: Train staff to prompt satisfied customers at checkout or when delivering the bill.

- Make It Easy: Place QR codes on tables, receipts, and takeout bags that link directly to review sites.

- Use Email & SMS Follow-Ups: After an online order or reservation, send a short message: "We hope you loved your meal! If you did, we'd appreciate a quick review. It helps small businesses like ours grow!"

- Host a Monthly "Review Spotlight" on social media, show-casing a featured customer review to encourage others.

> **Example: A café adds a "Review & Reward" system, offering a free coffee for every third review a customer leaves.**

Responding to Negative Reviews Professionally

Negative reviews can be opportunities for growth, but how you respond matters more than the complaint itself.

- Stay Calm & Professional: Never argue. Instead, acknowl-edge the issue, apologize, and offer a resolution.

- Take It Offline: If a review is particularly harsh, reply pub-licly and offer to resolve the issue via phone or email.

- Show Willingness to Improve: Customers respect busi-nesses that own their mistakes. A good response ex-ample: "We're truly sorry your experience didn't meet expectations. We value your feedback and would love to make it right. Please reach out so we can learn how to improve."

> **Example: A pizzeria receives a complaint about long wait times. The owner responds: "We appreciate your feedback and sincerely apologize. We're actively improving service speed and would love another chance to serve you!"**

Responding to customer feedback to improve operations

Reviews provide valuable insights into what's working and what needs improvement. The best restaurants don't just read reviews, they act on them to enhance service, menu offerings, and guest experiences [3] [4].

Track Common Themes in Feedback

- Use tools like Google Alerts, Yelp Insights, or ReviewTrackers to analyze trends in customer sentiment.

- Identify frequently mentioned pain points (e.g., slow service, food quality issues, staff friendliness) and address them directly.

- If multiple guests complain about the same issue, it's time to fix it.

> **Example: A restaurant notices multiple reviews mentioning cold food. The kitchen manager investigates and finds a plating delay, leading to new processes for faster service.**

Turn Constructive Criticism Into Action

- Kitchen & Menu Adjustments: If reviews frequently mention that a dish is "too salty" or "too small," tweak recipes or portion sizes accordingly.

- Service Training: If multiple guests mention "rushed service", hold a team meeting to retrain staff on hospitality techniques.

- Improve Ambiance & Cleanliness: If reviews point out a noisy dining room or dirty restrooms, address those issues immediately.

> **Example: A café receives consistent feedback about uncomfortable seating. They invest in new chairs and mention the update in a social media post: "You spoke, we listened! Come try our comfy new seating—your coffee breaks just got cozier!"**

Using testimonials and reviews for marketing

Positive reviews are powerful marketing tools. By showcasing real customer experiences, restaurants build trust, increase engagement, and drive more reservations and orders [5][6][7][8].

Feature Reviews in Social Media Content

- Create weekly "Customer Spotlight" posts featuring a five-star review and a photo of the dish mentioned.

- Design short Instagram Reels or TikToks where staff

reads positive reviews out loud.

- Use carousel posts or Stories showing before-and-after reviews when improvements are made.

> **Example: A steakhouse runs a campaign: "See what our guests are saying!" with a reel of glowing Google reviews overlaid on mouthwatering dish photos.**

Add Reviews to Your Website & Online Menus

- Showcase top customer testimonials on your homepage.

- Embed Google Review widgets so visitors can see real-time customer feedback.

- Place best reviews on online menu pages (e.g., "The best burger I've had in years – John D.").

> **Example: A fine dining restaurant adds "Guest Reviews" to each menu section: "The seafood pasta is incredible—so fresh and flavorful!" - ★★★★★**

Turn Video Reviews Into Social Proof

Encourage happy customers to leave video testimonials, which feel more authentic than text reviews.

- Ask loyal customers to record a quick 15-second review at the table.

- Offer a discount or free appetizer in exchange for permission to share the video.

- Repurpose video reviews as TikTok, Instagram Reels, and YouTube Shorts.

> **Example: A café posts a TikTok video of a customer raving about their signature latte, captioned: "This might be the best coffee I've ever had. Try it for yourself!"**

Final Thoughts

Online reviews are one of the most influential marketing tools in the restaurant industry today. By actively encouraging positive feedback, responding to criticism with professionalism, and leveraging testimonials for marketing, restaurants can enhance their reputation and attract more diners. The key is to engage with reviews consistently, use feedback for growth, and showcase customer love in a way that feels authentic and compelling. Restaurants that master this strategy will see higher trust, better customer retention, and long-term success.

---

1. Park, S. Y., & Allen, J. P. (2013). Responding to online reviews: Problem-solving and engagement in hotels.

2. Souki, G. Q., de Oliveira, A. S., & Guerreiro, M. M. M. (2022). Do memorable restaurant experiences affect eWOM? The moderating effect of consumers' behavioral engagement on social networking sites.

3. Bilro, R. G., Loureiro, S. M. C., & Guerreiro, J. (2019). Exploring online customer engagement with hospitality products and its relationship with involvement, emotional states, experience, and brand advocacy.

4. Pham, N. P. (2023). Customer engagement with brand-related content on social media within the context of the restaurant industry.

5. Kim, B., & Velthuis, O. (2021). From reactivity to reputation management: Online consumer review systems in the restaurant industry.

6. Li, H., Liu, H., Shin, H. H., & Ji, H. (2024). Impacts of user-generated images in online reviews on customer engagement: A panel data analysis.

7. Kim, B., Yoo, M., & Yang, W. (2020). Online engagement among restaurant customers: The importance of enhancing flow for social media users.

8. Hao, F. (2020). The landscape of customer engagement in hospitality and tourism: A systematic review.

7. Investing in Employee Satisfaction: A Happy Team Means Happy Customers

7. Strategy Seven

Investing in Employee Satisfaction: A Happy Team Means Happy Customers

A restaurant is only as strong as its team. Today, retaining top talent is more challenging than ever, but restaurants that invest in their employees' satisfaction, growth, and well-being will gain a competitive edge. A happy, motivated team leads to better service, increased efficiency, and stronger customer loyalty, while high turnover results in higher costs, operational disruptions, and lower morale. By offering incentives, career development opportunities, and fostering a positive workplace culture, restaurants can build a team that stays, grows, and thrives.

How employee retention impacts your bottom line

Employee turnover is one of the biggest hidden costs in the restaurant industry. Each time a staff member leaves, it costs money to recruit, hire, and train replacements, not to mention the productivity loss during transitions. Investing in employee retention leads to higher profitability, better customer service, and a more consistent brand experience [1] [2] [3] [4].

The True Cost of Turnover

Losing an employee means spending time and money on:

- Hiring & Training: Recruiting new staff, onboarding, and training take time and resources.

- Lost Productivity: New employees need weeks (or months) to reach peak efficiency.

- Declining Service Quality: Constant staff changes lead to inconsistent customer experiences.

- Team Morale Drops: When employees see high turnover, they may feel less motivated to stay.

> **By retaining employees for two years instead of six months, you could save thousands in rehiring and training costs while maintaining a high level of service and consistency.**

The Financial Benefits of Long-Term Employees

- Higher Customer Satisfaction: Guests love seeing familiar faces and receiving service from experienced staff.

- Increased Efficiency: Long-term employees know restaurant workflows, customer preferences, and operational best practices, reducing errors and improving speed.

- Stronger Teamwork: A stable team fosters better communication and collaboration, leading to a more enjoyable work environment.

Offering incentives and career development opportunities

Employees don't just want a paycheck, they want growth, recognition, and opportunities to advance. Providing career pathways and incentives encourages staff to stay longer, work harder, and feel invested in the restaurant's success [5] [6].

Performance-Based Incentives and Perks

- Bonuses for exceeding sales goals, customer satisfaction ratings, or teamwork efforts.

- Flexible scheduling options to accommodate personal commitments and reduce burnout.

- Staff meals, discounts, or wellness programs to show appreciation and support well-being.

> **Try implementing an "Employee of the Month" reward, where top-performing staff get a cash bonus, a preferred schedule, and public recognition.**

Clear Career Growth and Promotion Paths

- Define steps for advancement, such as moving from server to shift lead to manager.

- Offer cross-training opportunities, allowing employees to learn different roles (e.g., a server learning bartending skills).

- Support external learning by reimbursing staff for culinary courses or leadership training.

> **Try creating an internal leadership program where employees can train for management roles, reducing the need to hire externally.**

Building a workplace culture that fosters loyalty

Beyond pay and benefits, a restaurant's workplace culture plays a huge role in employee retention. When staff feel valued, respected, and heard, they are far more likely to stay long-term and take pride in their work [7] [8].

Foster Open Communication and Feedback

- Hold regular team meetings where staff can share concerns and ideas.

- Conduct anonymous employee surveys to gauge workplace satisfaction.

- Encourage an open-door policy, where management listens and takes action on feedback.

> **Hold monthly check-ins with each staff member to discuss goals, challenges, and suggestions for improvement.**

Recognize and Appreciate Your Team

- Celebrate birthdays, work anniversaries, and milestones.

- Publicly acknowledge staff achievements through shoutouts, bonuses, or small gifts.

- Organize team outings or appreciation events to build camaraderie.

> **Try hosting an annual staff appreciation night, giving awards for "Best Customer Service," "Most Improved," and "Team Player of the Year."**

Final Thoughts

A restaurant's success is directly tied to the happiness and longevity of its staff. High turnover leads to increased costs, disrupted service, and low morale, while a satisfied team creates a stronger, more efficient operation. By offering competitive pay, career growth opportunities, and a positive work culture, restaurants can retain top talent and provide an exceptional customer experience. When employees feel valued, they don't just work for a restaurant, they become part of its success story.

1. Mitchell, T. (2024). Managerial Strategies to Increase Employee Retention in the Restaurant Industry.

2. Coleman Jr, J. W. (2018). Employee Turnover in Fast Food Restaurants: An Exploration of Employee Retention Practices.

3. Smith, J. D. (2018). Successful strategies for reducing employee turnover in the restaurant industry.

4. Murphy, K. S., DiPietro, R. B., & Rivera, M. A. (2009). Factors impacting turnover intentions and job satisfaction of restaurant managers.

5. Gorham, J. A. (2021). Employee Retention Strategies in the Quick Service Restaurant Industry.

6. Ruiz, C. A. (2017). Strategies to retain millennial employees at full-service restaurants.

7. Feinstein, A. H., & Vondrasek, D. (2006). A study of relationships between job satisfaction and organizational commitment among restaurant employees.

8. Kim, K., & Jogaratnam, G. (2010). Effects of individual and organizational factors on job satisfaction and intent to stay in the hotel and restaurant industry.

8. Harnessing the Power of Influencer and Food Blogger Collaborations

8. Strategy Eight

Harnessing the Power of Influencer and Food Blogger Collaborations

Social media influencers and food bloggers have transformed how restaurants attract new customers. A single viral post or well-placed recommendation can drive huge spikes in reservations, online orders, and brand awareness. Partnering with influencers isn't just about getting likes; it's about creating strategic collaborations that lead to real, long-term customer engagement. The key is to identify the right influencers, structure partnerships effectively, and turn influencer-generated buzz into repeat business.

Identifying the right influencers for your brand

Not all influencers are created equal. A partnership only works if the influencer's audience aligns with your target customers. Instead of chasing big names with massive followings, restaurants should focus on influencers who have high engagement, credibility, and a local or niche audience that matches their brand

Look Beyond Follower Count

A smaller, engaged audience often converts better than a massive but disengaged one. Key factors to consider:

- Engagement Rate: Are people commenting, sharing, and saving their posts?

- Authenticity: Do they post honest reviews and interact with followers?

- Niche Relevance: Do they focus on food, lifestyle, or local dining scenes?

> **Example: A 10K-follower micro-influencer in your city with high engagement may drive more foot traffic than a 100K-follower influencer with a general audience.**

Prioritize Local and Niche Food Influencers

Partner with local food bloggers, TikTok foodies, and Instagram reviewers who:

- Regularly post about restaurants in your area.

- Have followers who live near your restaurant.

- Feature cuisine types or dining experiences that match your brand.

> **Example: A vegan café benefits more from partnering with a local plant-based influencer than a general lifestyle blogger.**

Use Tools to Find the Right Fit

- Instagram & TikTok Search: Look for hashtags like #FoodieNewYork #BestEatsMinnneapolis.

- Influencer Marketing Platforms: Use Upfluence, Heepsy, or AspireIQ to find vetted influencers.

- Competitor Analysis: Check which influencers review competing restaurants and reach out to them.

Structuring partnerships for maximum return on investment

A successful influencer collaboration isn't just about getting a single post; it's about creating value-driven partnerships that generate real brand awareness, engagement, and customer visits.

Offer the Right Incentives

- Complimentary meals or tasting menus in exchange for content creation.

- Paid campaigns for influencers with a strong, proven track record.

- Exclusive first looks at menu launches or events to build anticipation.

> **Example: A restaurant invites five influencers to a VIP preview night before launching a new brunch menu, ensuring social media buzz before the official release.**

Set Clear Expectations and Deliverables

Ensure influencers know exactly what's expected before the collaboration begins.

- Content Type: Photos, Instagram Reels, TikTok videos, blog reviews?

- Posting Schedule: How many posts? When will they go live?

- Engagement Actions: Will they reply to comments and encourage followers to visit?

> **Example: A high-end steakhouse partners with an influencer to post one Instagram Reel, two Stories, and a written review in exchange for a premium dining experience.**

Track Performance Metrics

Measure campaign success using:

- Engagement Metrics: Likes, comments, shares, and saves.

- Website Traffic: Did visits spike after the influencer's post?

- Promo Code Redemptions: Offer a special discount (e.g., "Use code FOODIE10 for 10% off").

> **Example: A pizza place tracks coupon code redemptions from influencer-led promotions to measure direct conversions.**

How to turn influencer visits into long-term customer engagement

The real value of influencer marketing isn't just the initial buzz; it's turning that exposure into long-term brand loyalty [3] [4] [5] [6] [7] [8].

Repurpose Influencer Content for Ongoing Promotion

- Repost influencer photos and videos on your restaurant's social media.

- Add influencer testimonials to your website and online menus.

- Use influencer-generated content in email marketing campaigns.

> **Example: A sushi bar compiles influencer clips into a highlight reel for Instagram, showcasing real customer experiences.**

Engage With the Influencer's Audience

- Reply to comments on the influencer's post to engage potential customers.

- Invite new followers to visit by offering a limited-time special.

- Encourage customers to tag your restaurant in their own posts for a chance to be featured.

> **Example: After an influencer posts a review, the restaurant comments and interacts with followers, answering questions about the menu and experience.**

Offer a Social Media-Exclusive Incentive

Capitalize on influencer traffic by giving new visitors a reason to dine in.

- Post a call-to-action such as, "Mention Melanie's post for a free appetizer" to track engagement.

- Launch a follow-up contest for customers to post their own experience.

- Create a hashtag challenge (e.g., "Show us your meal with #BestBitesBobsBurgers for a chance to win!").

> **Example: A café runs a "Foodie Feature" promo, where customers who tag the restaurant get entered to win a free meal.**

Final Thoughts

Influencer collaborations are a powerful way to drive brand awareness, increase foot traffic, and engage with new audiences. By choosing the right influencers, structuring partnerships effectively, and turning influencer-generated buzz into long-term engagement, restaurants can build a sustainable social media presence that continuously attracts new customers. The key is to go beyond a one-time promotion and use influencer partnerships as an ongoing growth strategy to build credibility, excitement, and customer loyalty.

---

1. Mohammad, N. F. B., & Mohamad, M. A. B. (Year not specified). The Effects of Influencer Personality and Social Media Content Towards Customer Purchase Intention in the Restaurant Industry.

2. Roobsawangkullapong, S. (2024). The Study of Social Media Marketing, Influencer Marketing, and Service Marketing Mix, Effecting Purchase Behavior of Online Food Services of Customers in Bangkok.

3. Lee, P. Y., Koseoglu, M. A., Qi, L., Liu, E. C., & King, B. (2021). The Sway of Influencer Marketing: Evidence from a Restaurant Group.

4. González, D. M. (Year not specified). Effects on People's Purchase Intention Caused by Influencer Marketing in the Restaurant Industry.

5. Philip, A. M., Othman, Z., & Talib, A. H. (2024). Social Media Influencer (SMI) Restaurant Reviews and Students' Patronization Decision.

6. Zhou, Y. (2019). Social Media Influencers and Their Marketing Effects on Followers: An Exploratory Study in Restaurant Review Microblogs.

7. Dinc, L. (2023). The Influence of Social Media Influencers on Consumers' Decision Making of Restaurant Choice.

8. Zhang, L., & Wei, W. (2021). Influencer Marketing: A Comparison of Traditional Celebrity, Social Media Influencer, and AI Influencer.

9. Financial Management: Keeping Cash Flow Healthy

9. Strategy Nine

Financial Management: Keeping Cash Flow Healthy

A restaurant's financial health is just as important as its food and service. Today, small restaurant owners must navigate rising costs, labor expenses, and economic fluctuations while ensuring steady cash flow and profitability. Poor financial management can lead to operational inefficiencies, cash shortages, and even business failure. To stay resilient, restaurants must track their finances carefully, avoid common financial pitfalls, and plan ahead for seasonal and economic shifts.

Common financial pitfalls for small restaurant owners

Many small restaurant owners focus on daily operations but overlook financial red flags until it's too late. Avoiding common financial mistakes can be the difference between thriving and struggling [1] [2].

Poor Cash Flow Management

Cash flow is the lifeblood of a restaurant. Many businesses fail because they run out of cash, even if they're making sales.

- Failing to budget for slow months can lead to missed payroll or overdue rent.

- Spending too much on upfront inventory can create cash shortages.

- Relying too heavily on credit without a repayment strategy can lead to crippling debt.

Solution: Maintain a cash reserve to cover at least 3-6 months of expenses and use a rolling cash flow forecast to anticipate shortfalls.

Underpricing Menu Items

- Many restaurant owners set menu prices too low to attract customers but fail to cover costs.

- Prices should reflect food costs, labor, rent, and overhead expenses.

- Failure to adjust for inflation, supplier price hikes, and changing market demand erodes profit margins.

Solution: Conduct regular menu pricing reviews and use a food cost percentage formula (targeting 28-35%) to price dishes profitably.

Not Monitoring Financial Reports

Many small restaurant owners don't review financial reports regularly, leading to overspending and missed profit opportunities.

- Ignoring profit & loss (P&L) statements can cause unnoticed financial losses.

- Not tracking cost per dish results in wasted money on high-cost, low-margin items.

- Overlooking payroll expenses can lead to unsustainable labor costs.

> **Solution: Use POS-integrated financial software like QuickBooks, Xero, or Restaurant365 to track profitability and spending in real time.**

How to track profitability and reduce unnecessary expenses

Smart financial tracking helps restaurant owners make data-driven decisions that improve efficiency and profitability [3][4][5][6][7][8][9].

Use Financial Metrics to Monitor Performance

To understand your financial health, track:

- Prime Costs (Food + Labor): Should be below 60% of revenue for sustainability.

- Gross Profit Margin: Should stay above 65% to ensure operational success.

- Break-Even Point: Calculate how much revenue you need daily to cover all expenses before making a profit.

> **Example: A café tracks its prime costs and sees labor creeping up to 45% of revenue, signaling the need for scheduling adjustments.**

Cut Operational Waste Without Sacrificing Quality

Reducing costs doesn't mean cutting corners, it means eliminating waste and inefficiencies.

- Optimize portion sizes to prevent food waste.

- Negotiate better supplier contracts for bulk discounts.

- Monitor energy usage and switch to energy-efficient equipment.

- Reduce paper waste by switching to digital menus and order systems.

> **Example: A restaurant trims costs by adjusting portion sizes on low-selling dishes, saving $1,500/month in wasted ingredients.**

Automate Financial Tracking to Save Time

Manual bookkeeping leads to errors and wasted time. Automating financial processes helps:

- Track expenses, revenue, and profits in real time.

- Send automated reports to track weekly and monthly performance.

- Identify seasonal revenue trends to predict slow periods.

> **Example: A bistro implements cloud-based POS and accounting software, reducing bookkeeping time by 10 hours per week.**

Planning for seasonal fluctuations and economic downturns

Restaurants face seasonal revenue swings and unpredictable economic shifts. Planning for slow periods and market changes is crucial for long-term success.

Forecast and Prepare for Seasonal Slumps

- Identify slow months (e.g., post-holiday January or mid-summer for urban restaurants).

- Build a seasonal marketing plan to attract customers during slower periods.

- Offer limited-time menu specials or promotions to boost traffic.

> **Example: A beachfront restaurant saves 15% of peak-season profits to cover winter operating costs.**

Diversify Revenue Streams to Stay Profitable

If foot traffic declines, other income sources can keep revenue steady:

- Offer catering services to expand beyond in-house dining.

- Develop takeout-friendly meal kits for at-home customers.

- Partner with corporate clients for recurring lunch orders.

> **Example: A fine-dining restaurant launches a holiday catering menu, adding an extra $50,000 in seasonal revenue.**

Maintain an Emergency Fund for Economic Downturns

- Set aside 3-6 months of operating expenses in case of unexpected downturns.

- Apply for lines of credit when business is strong, so funding is available when needed.

- Continuously monitor industry trends to anticipate shifts in consumer spending.

> **Example: A restaurant that had a financial cushion during an economic downturn was able to offer discounts without affecting long-term stability.**

Final Thoughts

Financial management is the backbone of a successful restaurant. By avoiding common pitfalls, tracking profitability, and preparing for seasonal shifts, restaurant owners can maintain healthy cash flow and long-term sustainability. Those who plan ahead, optimize expenses, and use smart financial tracking tools will have a clear advantage in a competitive industry. A financially stable restaurant is one that can adapt, grow, and continue delivering exceptional dining experiences for years to come.

1. Lai, H. B. J., Karim, S., Krauss, S. E., & Ishak, F. A. C. (2019). Can restaurant revenue management work with menu analysis?

2. Thompson, G. M. (2010). Restaurant profitability management: The evolution of restaurant revenue management.

3. Tyagi, V. S., Bhardwaj, S., Tyagi, S., & Tyagi, M. (2024). Food restaurant management system.

4. Dopson, L. R., & Hayes, D. K. (2019). Food and beverage cost control.

5. Tsai, H., Pan, S., & Lee, J. (2011). Recent research in hospitality financial management.

6. Harris, P. (2010). Profit planning.

7. Gumbo, M., & Sukdeo, N. (2024). Measures and challenges of cost control in fast casual restaurants: Case of Johannesburg, South Africa.

8. Kimes, S. E. (2008). The role of technology in restaurant revenue management.

9. Harris, P. J., & Mongiello, M. (2006). Accounting and financial management: Developments in the international hospitality industry.

10. Standing Out With Unique Dining Experiences

10. Strategy Ten

Standing Out With Unique Dining Experiences

These days a great meal isn't enough, customers crave unique and memorable dining experiences. With increased competition and social media driving food trends, restaurants must find ways to stand out beyond the menu. From themed nights and interactive dining to live entertainment and exclusive chef experiences, experiential dining keeps customers engaged, drives word-of-mouth marketing, and turns one-time guests into loyal patrons.

Themed dining nights and interactive experiences

Themed events add excitement and exclusivity to a restaurant's atmosphere, creating a reason for customers to visit outside of typical dining hours. When done right, they boost reservations, increase social media buzz, and build a community of repeat diners [1,2].

Seasonal and Holiday-Themed Nights

- Valentine's Day Date Night with a prix-fixe menu and candlelit tables.

- Halloween-Themed Dinners with spooky cocktails and staff in costume.

- Farm-to-Table Dinners featuring seasonal, locally sourced ingredients.

> **Example: A steakhouse hosts a Black & White Masquerade Dinner, requiring formal attire and featuring a specialized tasting menu, drawing high-value diners looking for a luxury experience.**

Interactive Dining Concepts

Customers want more than just a meal, they want to participate in the experience.

- DIY Hot Pot or Korean BBQ Nights where diners cook at their tables.

- Tableside Cocktail Crafting where bartenders mix drinks in front of guests.

- Build-Your-Own Pizza or Burger Nights with customizable ingredients.

> **Example: A sushi restaurant introduces "Roll Your Own Sushi" nights, giving guests fresh ingredients, professional guidance, and a fun, interactive experience.**

Mystery and Immersive Dining Events

- Murder Mystery Dinners where guests participate in a live, theatrical performance.

- 1920s Speakeasy Nights with hidden entrance passwords and vintage cocktails.

- Anime, Movie, or Fandom-Inspired Dinners featuring themed menus and decor.

> **Example: A café creates a "Harry Potter-Inspired Feast", serving Butterbeer lattes, wizard-themed desserts, and Hogwarts house-colored cocktails, selling out every event night.**

How experiential dining can drive word-of-mouth marketing

Dining experiences that spark conversation and social sharing create powerful word-of-mouth marketing both in-person and online. Unique experiences encourage guests to post photos, write reviews, and recommend your restaurant to others [3][4][5][6][7].

Creating Instagram-Worthy Moments

- Unique plating and presentation (e.g., dry ice effects, tableside flambé, oversized milkshakes).

- Themed decor and neon signs designed for social media photos.

- Surprise elements like hidden menu items, chef pop-ups, or personalized touches.

> **Example: A dessert bar serves a "Galaxy Dome" chocolate sphere that melts when warm caramel is poured over it, making it a must-capture moment on Instagram and TikTok.**

Exclusive, Limited-Time Experiences

Scarcity creates demand. Special dining events and pop-ups drive urgency and boost attendance.

- One-Night-Only Chef Collabs featuring guest chefs and unique dishes.

- Secret Menu Access for loyalty program members.

- Limited-Seating Themed Dinners requiring advance reservations.

> **Example: A fine-dining restaurant launches a once-a-month "Blind Tasting" menu, where guests don't know what they'll be served until they arrive, creating excitement and intrigue.**

Encouraging Customer Participation

- Feature a "Diner's Choice" Dish, allowing guests to vote on next month's special.

- Reward customers who share and tag your restaurant on social media.

- Offer a "VIP Experience Giveaway", where guests who engage online get entered to win a special dining package.

> **Example: A seafood restaurant runs a "Lobster Feast Challenge", where diners who finish a 5lb lobster meal get a photo on the Wall of Fame, driving repeat visits from competitive foodies.**

Incorporating live entertainment, cooking classes, or chef's table experiences

Bringing live entertainment and interactive chef experiences into your restaurant can create an unforgettable atmosphere that attracts new customers, boosts spending, and keeps guests coming back [8] [9].

Live Music, Comedy, and Performance Nights

- Jazz, acoustic, or DJ nights for an upscale ambiance.

- Live comedy or spoken word performances for a lively, engaging night out.

- Dinner & Dance Events featuring salsa, tango, or live cultural performances.

> **Example: A Latin restaurant hosts weekly Salsa Nights, offering guests a dance floor, live music, and a special mojito & tapas menu, attracting a new, dance-loving crowd.**

Cooking Classes and Interactive Chef Experiences

Bringing customers into the kitchen enhances their appreciation for the craft and builds stronger restaurant loyalty.

- Hands-on pasta-making classes led by the head chef.

- Wine and food pairing workshops in collaboration with local wineries.

- Baking and dessert decorating events for families and kids.

> **Example: A farm-to-table restaurant offers a "Harvest to Table" experience, where guests pick fresh ingredients from a garden and cook them with the chef, creating an educational and memorable dining moment.**

Chef's Table and VIP Dining Experiences

For high-end, exclusive experiences, offer intimate chef's table dinners where guests:

- Sit in a private setting with the chef explaining each course.

- Enjoy customized tasting menus unavailable to regular diners.

- Experience a behind-the-scenes look at your kitchen and culinary techniques.

> **Example: A fine-dining steakhouse introduces a 10-seat, once-a-week Chef's Table experience, featuring a multi-course menu, wine pairings, and direct interaction with the chef, priced at a premium for an exclusive, personalized night.**

Final Thoughts

Memorable dining experiences set successful restaurants apart from the competition. Whether through themed nights, immersive dining, live entertainment, or interactive chef events, offering something unique gives customers a reason to visit, share, and return. Restaurants that invest in experiential dining create lasting customer connections, increase word-of-mouth marketing, and build a strong, loyal community. A great meal may satisfy a customer for a night, but an unforgettable experience keeps them coming back.

---

1. Simpson, R. J. (2003). Theme and experience in restaurant design: A theory.

2. Beardsworth, A., & Bryman, A. (1999). Late modernity and the dynamics of quasification: The case of the themed restaurant.

3. Danhauser, R., Boechat, A. C., & Inácio, A. I. (2025). Eatertainment: Staging food and experiences for brand competitiveness in restaurants.

4. Wu, H. C., & Hussein, A. S. (2024). Exploring the drivers of experience relational outcomes among eatertainment restaurant customers

5. Ma, F., DiPietro, R. B., Li, J., & Harris, K. J. (2023). Memorable dining experiences amidst the COVID-19 pandemic.

6. Norris, C. L., Russen, M., & Taylor, S. Jr. (2023). Expanding the experiential value scale to predict independent restaurant dining intent.

7. Josiam, B. M., & Henry, W. (2014). Eatertainment: Utilitarian and hedonic motivations for patronizing fun experience restaurants.

8. Batat, W. (2021). How augmented reality (AR) is transforming the restaurant sector: Investigating the impact of "Le Petit Chef" on customers' dining experiences.

9. Cao, Y., Li, X. R., DiPietro, R., & So, K. K. F. (2019). The creation of memorable dining experiences: Formative index construction.

Bonus: Your 30-Day Action Plan

11. Bonus: Your 30-Day Action Plan

Implementing Proven Strategies for Restaurant Growth

This step-by-step action plan will help you implement the proven strategies from this book, simply and easily. Each task is designed to be manageable, ensuring steady progress without overwhelm.

How to Use This Plan

1. **One simple action per day** – No overwhelm, just steady progress.

2. **Adjust as needed** – If one strategy isn't a fit for your restaurant, swap it out. If the plan is too aggressive, slow it down. If its not challenging enough speed it up.

3. **Track your success** – Keep a log of what works best and refine over time.

Week 1: Understanding Your Market & Optimizing Your Menu

Focus: *Identify your target audience, analyze trends, and refine your menu for profitability.*

Day 1: Research local dining trends and customer preferences (Google Trends, Yelp, competitor menus).

Day 2: Define your ideal customer profile based on demographics, spending habits, and dining behaviors.

Day 3: Analyze your best-selling and lowest-performing menu items to determine what's working.

Day 4: Adjust pricing for high-margin items and remove underperforming dishes.

Day 5: Design a visually optimized menu that highlights bestsellers and profitable items.

Day 6: Test a small menu special featuring a seasonal or limited-time item.

Day 7: Gather customer feedback on the menu changes and make necessary tweaks.

Week 2: Social Media & Influencer Marketing

Focus: *Strengthen your digital presence and attract new customers through social media and influencers.*

Day 8: Optimize your Google Business Profile with updated photos, menus, and hours.

Day 9: Identify 3-5 local food influencers who align with your brand and audience.

Day 10: Create a list of potential influencer collaborations (e.g., free tasting in exchange for a post).

Day 11: Post a behind-the-scenes video on Instagram Reels or TikTok.

Day 12: Engage with local foodie communities on Facebook and Instagram by commenting and sharing content.

Day 13: Launch a customer-generated content challenge (e.g., "Tag us in your foodie photos to be featured!").

Day 14: Schedule a collaboration with an influencer or blogger for the coming weeks.

Week 3: Automation, AI & Employee Engagement

Focus: *Improve efficiency, reduce costs, and enhance employee satisfaction using technology and better workflows.*

Day 15: Research automated reservation systems if you don't already have one.

Day 16: Research POS-integrated financial tracking tools (like Toast, Square, or QuickBooks).

Day 17: Review and adjust your employee scheduling based on peak hours and labor costs.

Day 18: Identify one manual process (e.g., inventory, ordering) that can be automated and research tools to improve it.

Day 19: Conduct a 15-minute team check-in to gather employee feedback.

Day 20: Offer a small incentive (free meal, bonus) to recognize top-performing staff.

Day 21: Post a team spotlight on social media to showcase your employees and their contributions.

Weeks 4 & 5: Customer Engagement & Revenue Expansion

Focus: *Strengthen customer relationships, boost online reviews, and explore new revenue streams.*

Day 22: Respond to at least 5 recent online reviews (Google, Yelp, TripAdvisor).

Day 23: Design a customer loyalty program or improve your existing one.

Day 24: Plan a limited-time themed dining event (e.g., trivia night, wine pairing dinner).

Day 25: Send a follow-up message to recent customers, thanking them for their visit.

Day 26: Test a new add-on or upsell strategy (e.g., suggest wine pairings or dessert specials).

Day 27: Reach out to a local business for a potential cross-promotion or partnership.

Day 28: Offer a VIP experience or chef's table night to attract high-spending diners.

Day 29: Evaluate which strategies worked best so far and adjust your approach accordingly.

Day 30: Celebrate your progress and set long-term goals for continued growth!

Final Step: Take Action

The hardest part of business growth is getting started, but small, consistent actions lead to big results. Implementing this 30-day plan will set your restaurant up for increased revenue, stronger customer engagement, and long-term success.

Now it's time to take the first step. Let's get to work!

12. Final, Final Thoughts

Running a successful restaurant is about more than just serving great food, it's about staying ahead of industry trends, creating exceptional customer experiences, and managing your business with strategic precision. By implementing the proven strategies in this ebook, you're setting your restaurant up for sustained growth, increased profitability, and a loyal customer base.

Key Strategies for Long-Term Success

Know Your Market & Own Your Niche – Stay informed on customer preferences, optimize your menu for profitability, and build a strong brand identity.

Master Social Media & Digital Engagement – Use short-form video content, influencer partnerships, and user-generated content to attract new customers.

Leverage AI & Automation – Streamline reservations, ordering, and inventory management to save time, reduce costs, and enhance efficiency.

Strengthen Financial Health – Track cash flow, set smart pricing strategies, and plan for seasonal fluctuations to maintain steady profitability.

Create Unforgettable Dining Experiences – Implement themed nights, interactive dining, and live entertainment to drive word-of-mouth marketing and customer loyalty.

Invest in Your Team – A happy team means happy customers. Focus on employee retention, training, and workplace culture to build a strong, dedicated staff.

Expand Revenue Streams – Look beyond dine-in service by offering catering, hosting special events, and forming local business partnerships to maximize growth.

Now, It's Time to Take Action!

The strategies in this ebook are designed to be practical, actionable, and beginner-friendly. Success doesn't happen overnight, but small, consistent improvements will lead to big, long-term results.

Start by implementing your 30-day plan, one simple step each day will bring you closer to a more profitable, efficient, and thriving restaurant.

Stay adaptable and open to change. The restaurant industry is constantly evolving, and those who embrace innovation and customer-driven experiences will always have the competitive edge.

Your restaurant has the potential to stand out, grow, and succeed this year and beyond. The only thing left to do is take action because the best time to start is now.

Ready to Elevate Your Restaurant Business? Let's Do This!

About La Juana Whitmore Consulting

La Juana Whitmore Consulting was founded in 2014 on the belief that entrepreneurship is a powerful force for change, both for individuals and for the broader community. We understand that starting and growing a business is not just about making a profit; it's about pursuing a passion, creating opportunities, and making a lasting impact. Our firm was created to support those who dare to dream, providing the expertise, resources, and encouragement needed to turn those dreams into thriving businesses.

From our inception, we have been committed to walking alongside our clients, helping them overcome obstacles, seize opportunities, and achieve their business goals. Whether it's through strategic planning, financial management, or leadership development, we are dedicated to equipping entrepreneurs with the tools and confidence they need to succeed.

Today, La Juana Whitmore Consulting continues to build on this legacy, proudly serving a diverse range of clients and making a positive impact in the entrepreneurial ecosystem. Our vision remains as strong as ever: to see every entrepreneur equipped with the tools and strategies to turn their vision into reality.

Vision

A world where every entrepreneur is equipped with the tools and strategies to turn their vision into reality.

Mission

To be the strategic partner for small business owners, providing the expertise and resources needed to transform their business ideas into thriving enterprises.

Values

Integrity | Empowerment | Accountability | Resilience | Affluence

About Our Founder

La Juana Whitmore, MPNA, ASBC®, CFEI® is the founder of NextFemme Financial and La Juana Whitmore Consulting. She is a Business Strategist, Accredited Small Business Consultant®, Certified Financial Education Instructor℠, Doctoral Candidate, and University Professor who is passionate about designing and innovating business models for all types of companies.

In addition to an almost 20-year career with Target Corporation in business analysis, architecture, and strategy consulting, she has advised hundreds of small firms and nonprofits.

"At the heart of every successful business is a vision fueled by passion, strategy, and unwavering commitment. I believe that with the right tools and guidance, any entrepreneur can turn their dreams into reality."

La Juana Whitmore, MPNA, ASBC®, CFEI®

More Resources

Our Website:
LaJuanaWhitmore.com

FAQs and Glossary:
LaJuanaWhitmore.com/faqs-and-glossary

FREE Entrepreneur Toolkit:
LaJuanaWhitmore.com/free-stuff

LWC Shop:
shop.LaJuanaWhitmore.com

Our Consulting, Marketing & Speaking Services:
LaJuanaWhitmore.com/#services

NextFemme Financial (our sister company):
NextFemmeFinancial.com
Next-Femme.com